Advanced Marketing Techniques Anyone Can Learn

A Step By Step Guide of Advanced Marketing Techniques to Maximize Profits From Your Internet Business

By: TAK Technology LLC

ADVANCED MARKETING TECHNIQUES ANYONE CAN LEARN

TAK Technology, LLC
179 South Main Street
Gardner, MA 01440 U.S.A

ISBN - 978-0-9826947-1-8

Note: This book contains the opinions and ideas of its author. It is intended to provide helpful and informative material on the subject matter covered. It is sold with the understanding that the author and publisher are not engaged in rendering professional services in the book. If the reader requires personal assistance or advice, a competent professional should be consulted.

The author and publisher specifically disclaim any responsibility for any liability, loss, or risk, personal or otherwise, which is incurred as a consequence, directly or indirectly, of the use and application of any of the contents of this book.

Introduction

Hello! Thank you for your purchase of "Advanced Marketing Techniques Anyone can Learn". The techniques you find in this book are meant to further an already existing online business. If you do not have an online business yet we suggest you read "Internet Marketing Anyone Can Learn" to learn how to build an online business from the ground up.

Also, if you haven't yet I urge you read "Rookie Mistakes In Online Business Anyone Can Learn". If you don't you will be missing out on valuable information that will save you time and money. If you are having trouble, have questions, or are interested in learning more about a particular marketing technique.

Please contact us at - takteam@ourgrnbusiness.com.

Happy Reading!

Kristin and Tom

P.S. We would suggest you go through this book section by section slowly. There is a lot of information and it could get overwhelming if you try to jump in all at once. Each section is broken up into smaller sub sections so that you do not get overwhelmed.

Disclaimer

This book is designed to provide information on starting, launching, marketing, and building an online business. It is sold with the understanding that the publisher and author are not engaged in rendering legal, accounting or other professional services. If legal or other expert assistance is required, the services of a competent professional should be sought.

Advanced Marketing Techniques Anyone Can Learn is not a get rich quick scheme. Anyone who decides to start a business must expect to invest a lot of time and effort into it. For many people an online business is more lucrative than working a 8-5 job but you have to have the drive and motivation to build a solid, growing, rewarding businesses.

Every effort has been made to make this book as complete and accurate as possible. However, there may be mistakes, both typographical and in content. This book should be used only as a general guide and not as the ultimate source of Internet Marketing information. This book contains information on Internet Marketing and online business building that is current only up to the printing date.

The purpose of this book is to educate, the author and publisher shall have neither liability nor responsibility to any person or entity with respect to any loss or damage caused, or alleged to have been caused, directly or indirectly, by the information contained in this book.

Table of Contents

Chapter One

Add New Revenue Streams

1. Effective Upselling

A. What is an upsell?

If you apply the following technique to your website, you may see an immediate 20% to 30% increase in sales. What's great about it is it doesn't have to cost you anything and it will take you less than a few hours to implement. This great technique is called upselling. Fast food places have the upsell down to a fine art. You walk in their doors, head up to the counter, and focus in on their "Value Menu." You're looking for quick, cheap food. The cashier asks for your order and you tell him that you'd like Value Meal #0. They nod at your choice, and then pleasantly asks if you'd like that "Super-sized for only 49 cents." Only 49 cents? For more of fries and soda. That sounds like a great deal. You agree. And have bought into an upsell.

When a person trusts you and likes your product or service enough to buy from you once, they like you enough to buy from you again and again. The biggest obstacle you will face when persuading people to purchase from you is gaining their initial trust. This is why upsell products are so important. Remember the 80/20 rule? 20% of your customers are responsible for 80% of your profits. It's as easy as asking customers to "check this box" to claim Product X so they'll automatically receive the second product, and you'll automatically claim the extra profits.

One of the most effective places to include an upsell offer is directly on your order form. The customer has just purchased from you. Their credit card is out. You've already earned their trust and persuaded them to make a "buying decision." Now is a great time to make a second offer. The trick to making the offer work is ensuring that it's clearly related to the original purchase and offered at an appropriate price point. Make your upsell offers specially priced for customers buying that particular product at that exact moment only. Create a special one-time offer, don't let customers think they can decide later and come back.

Include text that says "Check this box to include Product X with this purchase at a special 20% discount." Then, in a couple of paragraphs, explain how Product X complements the product they're about to purchase, and how they'll benefit from having both. Clearly state the price of the product and make sure you mention your guarantee as well. Don't underestimate the power of the upsell. Once you've added it to your order forms, the sales all happen automatically.

You can also increase your sales by adding offers for complementary products to your purchase thank-you pages. When Bob buys a brand-new vacuum cleaner, the purchase thank-you page he sees might say something like, "Thanks for your purchase of a vacuum cleaner. Just in case you're interested, we also have this special stain remover available." This is such an easy thing to do, yet most website owners leave their customers high and dry after they purchase.

A customer is most resistant to buying in the moments before they decide to go ahead with their purchase. They're filled with doubt. "Do I really need this product?... Is it too expensive?... Will it be worth the money?" These are the questions that go through their minds before they buy. Right after they make a purchase, however, they feel much better. They're excited to start making use of whatever it is they've just purchased, and all that stress they felt before is gone. That's why a thank-you page can be another easy source of increased sales. If you sell upgrades or add-ons to your products, make sure you mention these on your "thank you" page. They've just demonstrated their willingness to buy one of your products... why not let them know about other products they might need?

B. Things to think about

So your customer has purchased your product, then hit your thank-you page and decided to grab your upsell offer as well. You'll likely send your customer an email confirmation of their order, right? Include another offer in your email. Now I know you may be thinking, Another? Isn't that getting too pushy? But it's not, the offers you include in your order confirmation emails should be soft offers and subtle suggestions, not hard sells like on your website. These confirmation emails present another excellent opportunity to take advantage of the relationship you've now developed with a new customer.

These people have a clear interest in what you offer. They trust you and they've already made the decision to buy from you once. They won't be irritated by another offer, they'll be thankful for the advice if you can position your offer as a complementary product or service that will help them in some way that is related to their initial purchase. A one-time customer is a lifetime customer if you play your cards right. Keeping your customers informed and presenting them with the solutions they need is half the battle. Solve their problems for them and they'll continue to purchase from you in the future.

2. Starting an Online Forum

A. Advantages of letting your visitors interact

Community-building features, such as discussion forums, have been popular on the Web for a while, especially on noncommercial and advertising-supported sites. These forums allow visitors to post and respond to messages on topics related to the website but even if the main purpose of your site is to sell goods or services, encouraging your visitors to interact with one another can have some benefits -

a. Build up community

Shopping on the Internet can be an impersonal experience at the best of times. By encouraging a community to form around your website, you immediately create a bond with your visitors. Your site becomes like a neighborhood, and people are likely to have a much more personal connection with it. That can make them more willing to buy from you, as you differentiate yourself from your competitors.

b. Get free content

By posting their own comments, your visitors are, in effect, creating free content. That means your site is constantly refreshed with content that would otherwise take ages to produce and might distract you from other tasks, like marketing.

c. Make your site stickier

As people use your forums, they'll be drawn back over and over again to read how others respond to their posts and to follow topics that interest them. While your return visitors are getting repeated exposure to your core products, they're also boosting your traffic significantly.

d. Customers can provide support through forums

If you've ever turned to the Web for support on a piece of software, you've likely found out how popular web forums are for providing support and advice. Not only do independent sites provide places where newbies can ask questions of more experienced users, but software companies have discovered that adding support forums can be an incredibly simple and free way of letting their senior customers support new customers.

Remember, since people come to the Web looking for information, they'll be attracted to your site more than to a competitor's site that's just trying to sell them something. The great thing about this is that people will come back to a well-run forum time and time again, because they form relationships with other visitors and the content is always fresh.

B. Promoting your forum

One of the challenges of growing a Web-based presence is that the value of your community is tied to its size and quality. On a community site your experience depends completely on how many other people are on the site and how closely their interests are aligned with yours. There's nothing as bad as coming to an Internet forum and finding that the few posts there are from months earlier. Visitors know there's no point contributing to the discussion, since hardly anyone comes through, and they'll move on without joining. It's better to avoid adding any kind of interactive community feature on your site until you have a substantial mailing list and your website traffic has increased. Here are some strategies for attracting members to your forum -

a. Announce and promote it to your opt-in mailing list

Make a point of mentioning your forums to your opt-in list. Even if people have already visited your site, they may not have noticed the forums or thought to visit them. Every time you send a mailing, mention the most popular threads and the latest topics, and invite people to drop by.

b. Tie it in to the rest of your site

Instead of having your forums as a separate part of your site, try to integrate them. You can set up forums with subjects that match your site's main sections or product categories, for instance, so you can promote them back and forth in a targeted way. If someone is on your site looking for a product they can reach the forum for that product with a click.

c. Feature the most popular forum subjects on your homepage

When you let people know what's being talked about, they're more likely to click through and join the discussion. You bring the content to them through the homepage instead of relying on them to check out the forums. It's also a good way to integrate the forums with the rest of your site.

C. Nurturing your forum

While forums can generate a momentum of their own, it does take some work to nurture and grow your forums. Think of it as hosting a social function: It's your job to set the right tone, welcome new guests, and make sure everyone gets along. The best way to recruit new members is by making sure the forums remain fresh, relevant, and civil. There are a few things you can do to keep your forums a great place -

a. Welcome new members

Take the time to welcome new members as they join the forum, since it can be intimidating for newbies to join in the middle of a conversation. One way is by providing a separate forum where new visitors can post their profiles.

b. Respond to messages and questions

Often people will post questions or comments about your site itself. Make sure you check your forums every day so you can quickly answer questions and let visitors know you're paying attention. If someone complains about a product they haven't been able to find, you can jump in and point them in the right direction on your site and get the sale.

c. Get the conversation rolling

As the forum owner, you're the one to get the ball rolling. Start with a general topic forum, and then watch what people talk about, and use that as a guide to launching new sections. You should start a new thread with a question aimed at your users, asking them to contribute their experiences or tips. In the beginning, it may also make sense to write some posts yourself to encourage others.

D. Get volunteers to help build your community

While forums can be a great source of free content, like any other gathering of people, they often require a host, or moderator. That means you need someone monitoring the postings, making sure people are posting on topic, and that no one's getting nasty or abusive. That doesn't mean you have to do all the work yourself. As your community grows, you'll discover natural leaders, the experienced members who post frequently and you can ask them to volunteer their time as moderators.

They will often feel honored to have been singled out. Chances are, they're so pumped about the topic and proud of the exposure that they'll gladly do it for free, or for a discount on some of your products. Plus, you can start inviting some of the more eloquent posters to contribute articles. Before you invite them to help, check out all of their posts to see how they have reacted to criticism or challenges. If they'll be acting on your behalf, consistency is important, so make sure your forum has clear rules posted for all users to see, and clearly explain your expectations of your volunteers.

Having a place for your visitors to communicate among themselves can be a powerful draw, but there are other benefits as well. It gives you the opportunity to listen in as visitors discuss topics and issues that interest them, and get a better understanding of their most pressing needs. It's like a built-in market research department that lets you keep your finger on the pulse of your community and your target audience. This can be a great source of ideas when it comes to developing other content. If you discover a thread that's been drawing a lot of posts, it may be a good topic to write an article on. If you find one of the regular posters has a good grasp on the topic, you could even approach them to write it for you.

If you find your visitors discussing a problem, a hard-to-find product, for instance, or a product that needs improving, it could open your eyes to a whole new opportunity to expand your business. Even if people aren't already talking about your product, you can invite comments. Set aside a forum to invite feedback and suggestions about your site, service, content, and products. You may get some negative comments, but it's a great way to find out exactly what your customers think.

If you decide to add a discussion board to your site, the first decision you have to make is whether you'll host the software on your own site or use a solution hosted by a third party, known as Application Service Providers (ASPs). Check with your web host, since some include the software you need to set up your own forums. Hosting the software yourself gives you more control over the look of the forums, and lets you integrate it into your site more completely. You may need help setting up the software for the first time, but it will also reduce your ongoing costs, since many ASPs charge a monthly fee.

As with other ASP tools, it's a good idea to avoid the free, advertising-driven discussion boards that are available. They usually don't offer enough customization to blend with the rest of your site, they display banner ads that aren't targeted to your visitors and they may not be as reliable as paid versions. To help you choose a good tool, visit some sites that have forums and join as a member so you can get a good sense of how they work and the features available. You can also send an email to the webmaster, asking how the software or ASP they use has worked for them.

Whichever route you choose, make sure you have full control over editing and deleting members' postings and moving threads that have been placed under the wrong topic. Here are a few of the more popular free forum software programs you can host on your own server. The one you choose will also depend on the type of server you're using, and which types of computer languages it can accommodate -

- **phpBB** (www.phpbb.com) - This free open-source bulletin board package uses the popular Hypertext Preprocessor scripting language and features a search function.

- **Invision Power Board** (www.invisionboard.com) - Also based on PHP, this solution is available as a free trial download or you can buy a Standard License for $149.99 (with a $25 renewal option after six months) or a Business License for $299.95 (with a $50 renewal option after six months).

- **IkonBoard** (www.ikonboard.com) - Offers a free download option, a one-time $39.99 install option, or priority support for $149.95.

Remember make users register for your forums so you can collect their opt-in email addresses and follow up with them later. Let them know that as a forum member they also qualify to receive your free newsletter, and include a link to your privacy policy.

E. A paid forum to create revenue

A forum that asks users to pay a membership fee is another powerful business model. It can increase your income from a one-time sale to a recurring revenue generator as members renew their subscriptions on a monthly or annual basis. Not all sites suit this kind of membership model. Successful paid forums all have one thing in common, sticky content that encourages people to visit again and again. If you're considering adding a paid forum to your site, you need to ask yourself if you have -

- A big opt-in list of subscribers
- A good response rate
- Good conversion rates
- An active customer base
- Lots of repeat visits to information-based content pages

Hostica (www.hostica.com) is a complete web host that offers many added services ideal for creating members-only paid forums, you will need some technical knowledge to get started. Some of the benefits and limitations of Hostica are -

Benefits -

- Good for creating forums

- Password-protects areas of your site and forum
- Templates for easy page creation

Limitations -

- Requires a lot of manual setup
- Hard to change passwords or user IDs regularly
- No way to automatically expel non-payers

Some other options for creating paid forums are -

- MemberGate (www.membergate.com)
- VisionGatePortal (www.visiongateportal.com)
- aMember Professional Membership Software (www.amember.com)
- Sentry Login (www.sentrylogin.com)

F. Things to think about

Only a small percentage of your first-time visitors will actually buy anything from your site, it's important to keep in contact with them. An opt-in list offering free information or a free newsletter is a key strategy. If you are focusing on a niche market that is passionate about what they do, adding discussion forums can be a powerful, inexpensive way to build a community and generate traffic. When mixed with a site selling related products, services, or information, a discussion forum can also be a way to bring visitors back so you can expose them to your products over and over again. It takes less work to run a forum than it does to produce the equivalent amount of fresh content, there is some time required.

3. Ad Space on Your Site

A. Google AdSense

You may already know that you can make money from your website by allowing other businesses to advertise on it. Fnding suitable advertisers and then selling the ad space and collecting the advertisers' payments takes a lot of time and effort. There is a way that you can create an extra revenue stream from your website through third-party advertising, without doing any of the work yourself. You may not be surprised that the solution comes from Google. It offers a service called Google AdSense (www.google.com/adsense), which allows you to make money from targeted text ads, paid for by Google AdWords advertisers.

These websites sell their own products and services and have their own content, but they are also AdSense "publishers", meaning that they've signed up for an AdSense account with Google to supplement their website's main source of revenues. As one of Google's AdSense publishers, you earn money every time a visitor to your site clicks on one of the text ads that appear on your page. The advertisers whose ads appear on your site have a Google AdWords pay-per-click account. They pay Google every time someone clicks on one of their ads. As an AdSense publisher, you receive an amount from Google every time a visitor to your site clicks on an ad on your web page. As the owner of the website that hosts the ads, you have a range of options that offer you some control over the ads that appear on your site. These include -

- Block competitive ads or other ads you don't want on your site
- Choose an alternative ad if Google can't generate a suitable one
- Choose where on your web page the ads will appear
- Choose different ad formats (like skyscrapers and banners) to display the ads
- Select the text and background colors
- Choose whether or not to have a border around the ads.
- Track your earnings
- Track and test the performance of different elements

The flexibility of the AdSense program -- as illustrated by the range of options listed above -- means you can ensure that the ads fit seamlessly into the layout of your website, rather than clashing with the existing content.

B. Potential benefits

AdSense isn't for every business but there are a number of benefits to testing

AdSense on your site -

a. Generate extra revenue

If you have a content-rich website with lots of pages containing information on specific topics, then AdSense is worth a look. Ads relating to the content on your website will be displayed. Visitors who arrive at your site will be searching for the information that you offer, so they should be interested in the products or services these ads offer. That increases the chances that people will click the ads and make you some extra cash. If your website contains content related to "big-ticket" items like holidays or electronic goods, then you are in an excellent position to generate a new stream of revenue.

b. Relevant ads might be appreciated

Displaying ads that complement the content of your site can provide a useful service to your customers. They may appreciate finding on your site information about associated products and services that they might not otherwise have come across. .

c. AdSense involves little effort

All you need to do is set aside a small area of your web page for the ads and paste the code that Google gives you into that space and Google does the rest, automatically generating different ads when a visitor lands on that page.

d. AdSense is free to join

There is no fee to join AdSense, and you can be earning revenues within minutes of being approved.

e. Rewards for sites that contain quality content

Content is becoming king again on the Internet. It's one of the best ways to achieve a high ranking in the free search engines. Fresh, relevant content keeps visitors on your site longer and keeps them coming back. If you run a content-rich information site or non-commercial blog, AdSense is worth a look as a way to generate some revenue.

f. You don't have to look for advertisers

Finding paying advertisers can be difficult, time-consuming, and ultimately not very lucrative, unless you have a site with very high volumes of suitable traffic. If you want to test third-party advertising on your website, AdSense takes away the need to try to find suitable advertisers, freeing you to work on other areas of your web business, like developing new products.

Many people believe that participating in AdSense can improve a website's ranking with Google. There is no evidence to suggest this is true, and Google denies it, stating categorically that this is not the case. In the absence of any conclusive research on the question of AdSense's impact on search engine rankings we can not answer the question one way or the other. There are many factors involved in determining your site's ranking in the various search engines, so you shouldn't base your decision on whether or not to use AdSense solely on the impact it may or may not have on the ranking of your site in Google, Yahoo, or other search engines.

C. Joining AdSense

Becoming an AdSense publisher is easy, go to www.google.com/adsense and fill out the online application. You'll need to check that your website complies with Google's policies (www.google.com/adsense/policies). Some content will make you ineligible for AdSense. Your site must be fully functioning, with easy navigation and no broken links. The policies also provide you with guidelines and restrictions on how and where ads can be placed on your website.

Once you've filled in the online application, Google will assess your site's suitability and get back to you within a few days. After that, you'll receive some code to paste into your website so you can start displaying ads and earning ad revenue. Google did not allow AdSense partners to disclose their earnings through the program. Now they can reveal their gross earnings, but not their click-through or traffic rates in relation to the program, or any other stats that Google might give them as part of their AdSense account. While you may not be able to predict accurately how much you can earn from AdSense, you can at least estimate what your potential earnings could be. These five strategies can help you make money through AdSense -

- Attract lots of high-quality traffic to your site
- Target high-paying ads
- Maintain good, keyword-rich content
- Ensure correct ad formatting and positioning
- Constantly track and test

Paying attention to these factors will help make AdSense a profitable tool for your business. There are a number of other things you can do to maximize your earnings-

a. Research keywords carefully

Research the high-paying keywords in pay-per-click search engines and use them in your AdSense pages. Bids can get as high as $12 to secure high rankings for some keywords, so targeting these is a great way to earn good AdSense income.

b. Ban competitors' URLs

You can get around the problem of promoting competitors' ads on your website by searching Google for URLs of competing sites and adding them to your AdSense filter. You could also try searching for sites that contain similar content to yours to get an idea of what ads could appear.

c. Create targeted, focused content

AdSense is ideal for content-rich sites. You can help Google target appropriate ads by sticking with one topic per page and keeping each article focused, increasing your chances of generating ads that are relevant to your content.

d. SEO techniques to attract high-paying ads

You can use search engine optimization techniques such as putting the high-paying keywords you want to target in the file name, the title, and the first 250 or so words on the page. These techniques are designed to help the search engines assess the relevance of your site to a user's search. Including keywords or phrases that people use to look for information on your subject area in your content helps your website achieve a higher ranking in the search results.

e. Place ads on text-heavy pages

These content-rich pages make it easier for Google to generate suitable ads. The ads tend to fit well into pages that contain lots of copy and don't have to compete with lots of other smaller elements on the page. You can even place AdSense ads "within" an article, letting the copy flow around the ad box as it would with an image.

f. Set up "alternate" ads

There may be occasions when Google can't generate an appropriately targeted ad for your page. Rather than display a blank space, you should make use of Google's alternate ads option, which allows a replacement ad or image to be automatically placed in the space if no AdSense ads are generated.

g. Don't place ads on pages crucial to your sales process

If your site is an e-commerce site don't place ads on pages that are crucial parts of your site's sales process.

h. Don't place ads on pages that contain lots of text links

Placing AdSense ads on pages that mainly contain lists of links will make it hard for the ads to stand out and those pages are not likely to attract highly targeted ads.

i. Use Google AdSense "channels"

Channels allow you to track the performance of your pages. They also allow you to carry out testing so you can refine your AdSense strategy based on analysis of the results. You can group pages together to assign them a channel, then test the performance of differing groups.

j. Review your stats and site stats regularly

Check the click-through rates of ads to see which pages and formats are performing well and monitor your channels. This way you can find out which ad formats work best and which pages on your site perform well attracting ad click-throughs.

k. Don't try to trick Google

Google is wise to any tricks, so you shouldn't click on ads on your page multiple times in an attempt to increase your revenue. Don't create pages and pages of unfocused content that have no reason for being there other than to generate AdSense ads.

D. Format and position

There are a number of AdSense options that give you control over where the ads appear on your web pages and what they look like. You are able to position an ad block, a section containing up to five ads, anywhere on your web page. You can choose from a variety of ad block sizes, and place up to three blocks on any one web page. You can also change the appearance, including colors and shading, of the text, links, background, and borders of the ads within the ad block.

Google offers a downloadable AdSense preview tool that allows you to see how the ads will look on your site in the various formats and color schemes. If you want to see samples of the kinds of advertisers that could appear on your site in the various formats that Google offers, visit http://adsense.toolbot.com, and just type in your URL. Google also introduced Link Units, a group of four or five links placed together on a page that can help AdSense publishers make the most out of limited space.

Each link brings the user to a page of advertisements. AdSense publishers are not paid for clicks on the initial links themselves, but are paid for clicks on the ads that are linked from those links. They are particularly effective for more focused content, where visitors tend to be seeking specific information. With all these options, it can be difficult to know which ones you should use. Here are some tips that can help you understand what will work for your website -

a. Format

Your choice of format will depend on how the ad blocks will fit into the layout of your web page and how much space you want to allocate to the ads. Many sites go for the skyscraper formats, where up to five ads are placed on top of each other down one side of a page. These are preferable to the banner formats, as people have become used to banner ads and are more likely to ignore them. Check out www.google.com/adsense/adformats for samples of all formats and sizes.

b. Position

Look carefully at the design of your web page and decide how prominent you want the ads to be. The best position is usually the right-hand side of your page, and above the fold. Placing ads on the left-hand side is not considered a good technique, as people usually look for navigation links in that space. Ads placed at the top of the page above the top navigation bar can be missed by visitors. One AdSense position that is becoming popular is the center of the page, this position can be effective, as people are used to looking for content in the center of the page, so they are less likely to ignore the ads.

E. AdSense may not be for you

If you follow the strategies recommended above, AdSense can allow you to pull in at least some advertising revenue. Before getting carried away with the thought of making some easy extra money, you should be aware of the negative impact adsense can have on your business. Some of these are the very reasons why we do not use adsense in our business.

a. Display competitors' ads

Ads for your competitors will show up on your site. Advertising competing sites on your own site is not the best business strategy, and it's crucial that you assess how much of a risk this would be for your business. Google does let you ban up to 200 URLs at any one time. You need to regularly check the reports AdSense generates showing the URLs of ads that appear on your site, and keep your filter up to date.

b. You can't make a new window open when someone clicks on an ad

Google does not allow ad sites to be opened in a new browser window. When someone clicks on an ad on your site, they will leave your website completely and may never come back. You work hard to drive traffic to your website, and all that work can go to waste if a visitor sees an ad that catches their eye and gets caught up in the new website.

c. Draw visitor's attention away from your sales messages

If you sell products and services through your website, you don't want potential customers to be distracted from your sales messages. Even if a visitor clicks on an ad, leaves your site, and then comes back, they may have found something else to spend their money on, and not be so inclined to buy from your website.

d. Upset your existing advertisers

If you already sell advertising space on your site, your advertisers may resent the fact that they are paying you for the space on your site, when their ads could turn up anyhow through AdSense.

e. Ads could take up website space that could be used better

Your website is your online store, just as in a brick-and-mortar store, you should use all the space to try to generate sales. The space on your web page is the only opportunity you have to catch the eyes and wallets of visitors.

f. Unsuitable ad content could hurt your credibility

Google is fairly strict on who can and can't advertise through them. You may have stricter standards and, although you can ban URLs, there's always the chance that an unsuitable ad will show up on your site, damaging your reputation in the eyes of your customers and making them doubt your integrity.

g. Ads can clutter up your site

You need to pay attention to how you present the ads on your web pages, as they can make your web page look ugly or cluttered.

h. Ads of this type are everywhere

Targeted text ads are all over the Internet, they appear on Google search results pages, on websites using AdSense, and even form part of Google's free email program. The result of all of this exposure is that, unless the ads are really attention-grabbing or relevant, people are starting to ignore them.

i. Working on AdSense takes up valuable time and you could lose money

If you're not careful, managing your AdSense account could distract you from time you should be spending on your real business.

F. Things to think about

AdSense can be a very useful extra source of revenue when used on the right website. AdSense is very easy to set up and costs nothing. Before diving into an AdSense account for your website, pay close attention to the potential pitfalls of the program and assess the impact they may have on your business.

Promoting competitor's sites, sending visitors away from your site, and displaying too many ads or unsuitable ads may distract visitors from your sales messages and hurt your bottom line rather than boost it. You also need to understand that you must achieve the right combination and regular tracking and testing.

If you think your business can benefit from AdSense, the best strategy is to test ads out on a page of your site for a set time and see what impact they have on your visitors and your bottom line. AdSense can certainly provide you with a stream of advertising revenue that would otherwise be out of reach for a small business, if you carefully monitor your site.

4. Sell Your Service Online

A. <u>How to sell a service?</u>

Do you want to sell a service on the Web? Many people make the mistake of thinking that a service business just isn't suitable for online business. An online service business can be very lucrative as long as you recognize a few key factors and implement a few important strategies. There are challenges to taking your service business online but we're going to show you how to overcome those challenges. We've also included the best ways to design your website and your salescopy for a service business on the Internet. As well as proven traffic-generation techniques you can use to grow your service business. So, How do you sell a service online? It's a good question because almost all selling and traffic generation techniques work equally well for both product- and service-based business models. However, there are a few challenges faced by those selling services -

a. You are the product

When you sell a service, you are the product, whether you're a doctor, lawyer, real estate agent, mechanic, hair stylist, trainer, whatever. You are the product, you're selling your time with the promise of a particular result, as opposed to selling a tangible product.

b. Your time is limited

Unlike someone selling a physical product that can be stored and shipped on demand, you can only provide as many services as your time allows.

c. Prove your ability to deliver measurable results

People will want to see proof that you've delivered great results for other clients but they will also want to know that you are flexible enough to meet their own unique needs. You must walk a fine line, making sure that you keep confidential client information confidential, while proving that you've satisfied the needs of other clients and demonstrating your ability to customize your service to meet their personal needs.

d. Using a global medium to attract local business

Service-based businesses rely on local clients, so sites that rely on local customers need to actively pursue sources of local traffic.

B. Techniques, tips, and strategies

a. Establish your credibility

When you sell a service, you are typically selling a relationship with yourself. This requires that you spend more time and effort establishing your credibility and developing a rapport with your visitors than is typically required on a site selling a physical product. So establishing your credibility, establishing your value, is important to closing the sale. You not only need to establish the benefits of the service you're offering, you need to establish the value of you providing this service.

b. Provide proof that others were satisfied with your service

Depending on the nature of the service you provide, you may choose to do this in a few different ways. Testimonials from clients or an online portfolio of your work are great ways. If the confidentiality of your clients is important, then you may need to approach this a bit differently by including more general descriptions of problems you've encountered and steps you've taken to solve them.

c. Be specific about what you're offering

This is a common mistake that website owners make, whether they sell a service or a product. You can never assume that providing information about what you've done for other clients will enable visitors to your site to make that leap and picture what you'll be able to do for them. You need to be specific about what you're offering -

- Look at other similar service providers
- Do you specialize in anything
- What kind of guarantee do you offer
- How will your services be delivered

Many times website owners fail to provide their visitors with enough information. Salescopy with a detailed breakdown of the services you provide, with the benefits you offer clearly explained, will be one of the most critical parts of your site.

d. Flexibility

People will not only want to see proof that you've delivered great results for other clients, they will want to know you're prepared to customize your service to meet their needs. Thorough salescopy that clearly explains how you're willing to customize your services will be very important.

e. Make it easy to contact you

If you're selling a service over the web then you are generating leads, your goal is to get visitors to contact you. Just as someone selling a product needs to make a seamless transition between their salescopy and their order form, you need to make a seamless transition between your salescopy and the point of contact. Provide an online form, email address, phone number, fax number, and any other relevant information. Make sure this information is visible and easily accessible from every page of your website.

f. Get listed in local directories

The location of your clients is important, while almost all of the traffic techniques used to drive visitors to product-based sites can be applied to service-based sites these few techniques are useful if you need local traffic -

- Network with other local businesses
- Get your site listed in local online directories
- Take advantage of sites like Elance.com

g. Encourage referrals and repeat customers

Always follow up with existing clients, email has made following up with your existing clients extremely easy and cost-effective, so there is no excuse for not following up and taking advantage of this source of easy extra income. Don't be afraid to remind previous customers that you're there and ask for referrals. If you've done a good job for someone, they'll likely be more than happy to refer friends and business associates to you. If you sell a service as your main revenue stream, you can also boost your income by offering products that are complementary to your service through your website.

C. Things to think about

When you sell a service over the web, you are going to solve visitors' needs and benefit them. Once you've gotten comfortable with this, everything else should be easy. Salescopy strategies, traffic generation, and website design strategies can be transferred directly to a service-based website to increase the leads you attract, the deals you close, and your online income.

5. Sell Licenses to Your Products

A. Offering reseller licenses

Have you heard the term "resell rights" floating around the Internet? Buying and selling licenses to resell products is one of the hottest business ventures going. You may have come across offers to buy these licenses or rights. Have you ever considered offering resale rights on your products? I know what you may be thinking. Why would you want to let other people sell your product or service and earn all the profits that could've been yours? Say you've spent months or years creating your product line, putting a sales process into place, developing valuable relationships with your customer base, and improving on different elements of your business.

When you offer rights to resell you're selling more than the rights to a product or service. You're also giving away your best sales materials, your salesletters and email promotions, and your marketing campaign for that one offer. If you have exhausted your market with a particular product and will not be selling updates or new versions of it to your customer base, you can sell resell rights for the product and then your customers can turn around and sell that product to their own customer base. Some of your customers already have lists of their own customers and that means they have access to markets you may not be able to reach. By giving them resale rights to your product, you can branch out to reach a much wider audience.

It's an attractive offer for your customers, because you are offering them a proven product that has already been demonstrated and proven successful in your market. You are likely giving them what is essentially a ready-to-go business plan with all the elements of a good marketing campaign intact. You'll be selling a business opportunity, so you can rightly charge a much larger sum for the resale rights than you would for the product itself. Your customers can turn around and sell your product over and over again for as long as they like, and can build an entire business for themselves from this one item.

If your product is a good one, they'll be willing to pay a relatively high price for the rights to resell it, knowing that just a small investment of time and effort will allow them to recover that initial investment quickly. Let's say you've been selling a popular eBook to your market for a year or two. The eBook is up-to-date and contains highly valuable information but your customers aren't ever going to buy more than one, and the sales on it have slowed down, no matter what tricks you pull out of your sleeve to try to promote it. You've been selling this eBook for about 50 bucks and it's done well for you. However, your market is saturated and you realize you need to branch out to other markets. It can take awhile to establish yourself in other markets, it may be good to sell the rights to your eBook and let your resellers approach those markets in which they are already established. You could charge up to $500 or so for the rights to this book, just 10 sales will make up the investment costs for your customer. By providing these materials, you'll be giving your resellers the tools they need to succeed. Do your best to include -

- Your salesletter
- The notification letter that you used to email customers to tell them about the eBook and direct them to the salesletter at your site
- Some tips and pointers about how to set up the ordering and download process

This means when your customers purchase the rights to your product, they are skipping the entire process of creating a product and finding the right sales techniques to sell it. As we all know, this process can take anywhere from a few weeks to a few months. The advantage to your customer is enormous, especially if they have a customer base with which they have already established a relationship. Plus selling the rights to resell your products is the opportunity to spread your name and reputation a little further abroad. By selling reprint rights, you're not just selling a license to your customers you're allowing them to resell your product to their customers. That means you have the opportunity to make yourself known to all of your customer's customers.

Take advantage of this opportunity wherever possible by including your company name on all your products. Include an "about us" in your eBooks, or add links to your website in your copyright information. You may even want to include mentions of your other products where appropriate, allowing your customer's customers to find out more about you and your business. If you're selling the rights to an eBook, you can even include links directly to your product sales pages. This is a way to increase your market reach and extend your offerings to a wider audience. Be sure to only recommend products where appropriate, and only alongside valuable information. Do not try to sell the rights to what amounts to a brochure or catalogue for your own business. This won't win you any customers of either reprint rights or the products you mention. Keep your product plugs subtle and sincere, recommend your own products and services only when you believe they are suited to the situation.

B. Write up a licensing agreement

Before you hand over the rights to your product, you'll need to protect yourself and your business by drawing up a licensing agreement that customers must agree to before purchasing your product. The agreement should be designed to ensure that your reseller is bound by a few restrictions, including -

- The minimum price for the product
- Your copyright restrictions, resellers should not be allowed to modify the content or format of your product or service
- Your company policy regarding spam
- Any other legal details you will want to include

Look over the legal agreements at sites selling similar products and compare theirs to yours. If you have a lawyer, make sure your lawyer takes a look at your license agreement. If you don't have a lawyer, consider purchasing legal forms designed for this use at a site like -

- www.findlaw.com
- www.weblawresources.com

Even if you use forms like these, it would be wise to have a lawyer take at least a quick look at your agreement to protect your business.

C. <u>Things to think about</u>

Offering reseller licenses to your customers may provide an unexpected avenue of growth and profitability to your business. When you're thinking about offering reseller licenses, think about who is likely to buy your product. The wider your market, the more potential success you are likely to have, as your customers, in turn, will be able to find interested people to sell to. When you begin to sell the rights to your product, you should immediately stop selling it yourself. There is just no way your potential customers will want to compete with you in a market that you know better than they do.

6. Super Affiliate

A. <u>How affiliate products could help you?</u>

If you want to start an Internet business but don't have a product or service of your own to sell, then promoting affiliate products to earn profits can be a great alternative. An affiliate program is a partnership where you promote another company's product or service on your website to earn a percentage of their sales. The company assigns you a special affiliate URL that tracks all of the visitors you send to their website and all of the sales that you generate. You earn a commission each time someone you've referred makes a purchase. There are many benefits to promoting affiliate products -

a. Gives you a product or service to promote if you don't have one

With affiliate products, you don't need to find, purchase, warehouse, or ship any stock. All you need to do is find a product appropriate for your target audience, and then find ways to draw people to your site and click through to the affiliate product.

b. One of the fastest ways to establish an income

Once you've researched the affiliate program that's right for you, you can establish the actual affiliate relationship in minutes. As soon as you've been approved, you can add the affiliate link to your website and start referring sales to their site. You probably won't start making lots of money right away but it does get an income stream started.

c. Don't require complex websites

You don't need to spend a lot of time or effort to get yourself set up as an affiliate marketer. A basic HTML web page is all you need to get started. You don't need to spend a lot of time setting up your website, you will have to devote time to marketing once it's up and running.

d. A good choice even if you already have a website

If you already have a website, with an established customer base and opt-in email list, then you're in a perfect position to begin promoting affiliate products and services. You can begin to significantly increase your income and capitalize on the lifetime value of your customers and subscribers by sending them backend offers of related affiliate products and services.

B. Super affiliates

It's hard work that separates a regular affiliate from a super affiliate, someone who markets the affiliate product like it's his or her own product, and makes a very successful living doing it. Super affiliates use smart marketing strategies to drive traffic to their websites, increasing the number of people who click through to the affiliate products and purchase them. They also work very hard to establish their reputations as credible sources of information about their products. It's the relationship of trust they build with their customers that sets super affiliates apart. Super affiliates -

a. Define a niche market and target their audience

Super affiliates know that not defining a niche market and targeting products to that market is one of the biggest mistakes Internet marketers make. People think that by promoting 10 or 15 different and unrelated products on their sites, they can make 10 times as much money. Your site just ends up looking like a flea market and is unsuccessful.

b. Build relationships with their visitors

Super affiliates work hard to be not just salespeople but trusted friends and advisors to their customers. They spend a lot of their time building relationships with their customers, providing them with important information and products they want to hear about.

c. Actively market their products

Super affiliates actively market their featured products. They know that posting a link to their affiliate sites and then sitting back and waiting for the profits to roll in is not a realistic approach. In order to market affiliate products effectively, keep track of who customers are, and follow up with them to make sure the customer understands the value of the products.

d. Have content-rich websites

Super affiliates know that the way to convert their visitors into paying customers is by giving them plenty of reasons to visit their websites. They develop content that people actually want and find useful, such as product reviews, comparisons, helpful tips, newsletters, and so on.

e. Perceived experts in a specialized area

Successful super affiliates know that they need to learn as much about their products as possible. They understand how important it is to speak with authority about what they're selling, and be able to anticipate every question a potential customer might have.

f. Test their marketing strategies

Super affiliates aren't content to stop working when they start earning a modest income. Once they get those first sales and know people are looking for what they're selling. They start looking for better ways to bring their products to people's attention.

A lot of people think they can post an affiliate banner on their site and they'll earn thousands. There are certain steps you need to take and rules you need to follow if you really want to maximize your affiliate sales. You need to -

a. Collect opt-in information

Contact information for your potential customers is gold. Armed with this information, you won't have to depend on the affiliate you're representing to market the product, you can market it yourself and you can do it actively by keeping your contacts informed of the latest developments concerning your products.

b. Give personal recommendations

Personal endorsements and testimonials are a powerful way to capitalize on the relationship you've already developed with your customers and subscribers. You've established yourself as a reputable, credible person with a considerable amount of expertise in your area of interest. When you personally recommend a product or service to your customers they will be more likely to consider making a purchase.

c. Provide lots of content

A website with virtually no content and a long list of affiliate banners is no use to anyone. If you want to attract visitors, and keep them long enough to send them to your affiliates, you'll need to give them good reasons to come to your site. Fill your website with relevant information that will help people make decisions about any products you recommend -

- Reviews of products
- Customer testimonials
- Helpful tips related to the product
- Guest articles

d. Sell relevant products

It's important that any product or service you recommend relates to the overall theme of your website. If it doesn't, you will end up damaging your credibility and decreasing your sales.

e. Drive targeted traffic to your site

Before you can make money promoting affiliate products, you have to get a reasonable amount of traffic to your site. Here are some ways super affiliates drive traffic to their sites -

- Search engine placement
- Articles on other websites
- Pay-per-click traffic
- Strategic linking
- Opt-in marketing

f. Test everything

If you want to maximize your affiliate sales and income, then you need to work at it and test everything. It's worth the time and effort. Once you've found a successful formula that is pulling maximum sales, you can sit back and put your business on autopilot.

C. Find affiliate programs

There's no end to the number of affiliate programs available for you to join. Not all of them are worth belonging to. You need to conduct some research to find the right affiliate program for your market.

a. Finding good affiliate programs

If you're looking for a reputable affiliate program to join, stick to the better-known affiliate directories and networks when doing your research. There are three places where you can look -

- Affiliate directories
- Affiliate networks
- Individual websites

b. Deciding if an affiliate program is good

There are lots of affiliate programs out there, not all of them are worth joining. Here are things to watch for -

- Quality of product or service
- What's the commission? (20% to 50% of the profit is a fair commission)
- Good reputation
- No exclusivity clause, make sure you read all contracts and agreements carefully

D. Things to think about

Becoming an affiliate is one of the fastest ways to start making money on the Internet. You don't need to find a product to sell or worry about paying for it up front, storing it, or shipping it. You don't need a complex website, or a lot of technical skill to get started. Becoming a super affiliate takes more time and work. A super affiliate earns a solid income by working full-time to promote affiliate products.

7. Shopping Bots

A. What is a shopping bot?

Shopping bots are like search engines except instead of finding information, they are designed to help shoppers locate the products or services they're looking for on the Internet. In the same way search engines provide searchers with links to websites, shopping bot sites list specific product information so shoppers can compare features and prices. Shoppers can search by product category or keyword to bring up a list of products from a variety of merchants. Many shopping engines allow searchers to compare characteristics such as price, product ratings, or customer reviews.

The term "bot" comes from the search engine "robots" that comb websites looking for information to index, in this case product and pricing information and direct links to the corresponding sites where consumers can make a purchase. They're popular with consumers, bots allow them to easily compare prices of the product they're looking for, saving them the time they'd spend looking through lots of individual websites to find the best price. Some shopping bots allow consumers to leave reviews for others to read about particular products.

Because shopping bots cater to people who are actively looking to buy, the traffic your website can attract through them is targeted and potentially valuable. This means that shopping bots can be an excellent way for you to promote your products, allowing your potential customers to find out exactly what you have to offer. Through shopping bots you can have -

- Cheap or free listings
- Exposure to consumers who are searching for your products
- Direct links from your listing to the relevant product page on your website

The search engines love these shopping portals because they're -

- Full of frequently updated product listings
- Full of keywords
- Valuable to visitors because of their comparison and review features

Popular shopping bots including Google Product Search, Yahoo! Shopping, and Shopzilla and should be a part of your Internet marketing plan. Shopping bots are a cheap and in some cases free way to gain extra exposure for your product. It is often easier and cheaper to rank at the top of categories in the shopping bots than in the search engines. Most shopping bot sites will display ads to potential customers in an appealing, easy-to-understand format.

If your product or service is competitively priced or offers buyers a unique or compelling benefit, and if you have a well-written ad, distinguishing yourself from your competition will be a piece of cake. Shopping bots can be a great place for business owners struggling to stand out in competitive markets to capture the eyeballs of qualified potential customers and as these potential buying customers are often in full-on buying mode, the return on investment can be significant.

B. Get registered with shopping bots

Although one shopping bot site differs slightly from the next, registering your website and products with most of them is pretty easy. Here are the basic rules -

a. Which shopping bot formats are right for you

There are dozens of shopping bots to choose from but there are only a few that get enough traffic to make submission worth your time. What you want to determine is whether your products or services are competitively priced or whether they have a feature that sets them above the competition. Some shopping bot sites list products according to price or give shoppers the ability to modify a search. Others will list suppliers in priority sequence based on pay-per-position bidding. Shopping bots that place a strong emphasis on price may not be favored by business owners who rely on a unique selling feature.

b. Determine cost of placing your ad

On the majority of shopping bot sites, you will be expected to pay on a pay-per-click (PPC) basis. On average, these cost between 5 cents and $1.25 per click, depending on the popularity of your product and the category it appears in. You will also need to make a deposit of between $100 and $200, depending on the product or service you are selling.

c. Get your product feed ready to go

Your product feed is the information you submit to a shopping bot about the product you want advertised. This may include the description of your product, pricing, the category you want it to appear in, your website URL, and product availability. When creating your product descriptions, be sure they include clear benefits, this can make the difference between having prospective customers find you with ease or your ad getting lost or pushed down in the search results. Try to avoid using abbreviations or product codes in your ad. You only have a few seconds to grab a consumer's attention and direct them to your website. If you sell a product that has a number of competitors all within a similar price range, then remember to stress any unique benefits that you offer.

How you submit your product feed to a shopping bot site will vary depending on the guidelines of the site. Some sites make it easy to submit your feed through their online forms or downloadable software; other sites make it a bit of chore to submit your feed, requiring you to upload information through an FTP client. Whatever type of product feed a site uses, beware of third-party companies or websites that want to take your hard-earned money to create product feeds for you.

d. Register your product feed

Once you have decided which shopping bot site to use and have created your product feed, registering should take a matter of minutes. The shopping bot site administrators will review your information and product feed for approval. Be aware that the approval process can take anywhere from a few days to a couple of weeks. Larger shopping bot sites share their listings with affiliated sites. So when registering with a shopping bot site like shopping.com, which is affiliated with dealtime.com and epinions.com, will get you listed with the affiliated sites at no extra cost.

e. Get top listings in the shopping bots

Here are the main ways you can get your site to rise to the top of the shopping bots -

- Pay for an enhanced listing
- Compete on price
- Boost your merchant/user rating
- Optimize your product listings for relevant keywords

There are many shopping bots on the Internet. All of them fall into three categories-

- Commission-based, where you pay a fee for every transaction
- Pay-per-click, based on a charge per click-through to your site
- Free

Let's take a look at some of the biggest and best shopping sites –

a. Shopzilla

Shopzilla requires a $50 deposit from its merchants that will be applied toward your cost per clicks. It offers low minimum bidding rates, starting at just 10 cents per click and moving up to 30 cents per click. Product feeds submitted to Shopzilla may take seven to 14 days to be listed. Shopzilla's network includes BizRate.

How sites are ranked - Shopzilla looks at pricing, merchant reputation, product popularity, and product availability to determine how search results are listed.

Top ranking strategies - Pay for better placement and optimize your data feed.

What you'll pay - $.05 to $1 per click.

b. PriceGrabber

PriceGrabber offers many of the same features as Shopzilla, with one difference , merchants without a website can use PriceGrabber's "Storefront" option to post their products or services.

How sites are ranked - Sites in the search results can be ranked according to the shopper's preference.

Top ranking strategies: Pay for better placement and optimize your data feed.

What you'll pay: Merchants are charged $1.50 plus 6.75% of the selling price on each sale. You must also pay a monthly listing fee of $0.10 per active product. .

PriceGrabber also hase a pay per click model that allows merchants with websites to list their products on PriceGrabber. The merchant then pays every time a user clicks on their product offer.

c. Shopping.com

Shopping.com is a popular eBay-owned website. It works well for merchants who don't want to spend time coming up with catchy product descriptions for their product feed because Shopping.com displays a universal description of commonly searched items at the top of a search page, with ads listed below. Shopping.com offers a flexible bid-management system. A minimum prepayment of $700 is required to get started as a Shopping.com merchant.

How sites are ranked - Search results come from matching a search term with a product description. Stores bid for enhanced placement on certain product results.

Top ranking strategies: Pay more per click, compete on price, and boost your trusted store rating.

What you'll pay: You'll pay $.05 to $1 every time someone clicks through your product listing to your website.

d. Yahoo! Shopping

Yahoo! Shopping is the largest shopping site and has been recognized as one of the largest multi-category commerce destinations on the Web.

How sites are ranked - Search results are listed by item type but not necessarily by manufacturer or model number.

Top ranking strategies - Pay for better placement and compete on price.

What you'll pay - Costs start at 15 cents and go up to $1.

e. Google Product Search

Google Product Search is a free service where sellers can list goods for sale two ways -

- Filling out their online form for an individual item
- Setting up a data feed to submit listings for multiple products

How sites are ranked - Results are compiled by the same software Google uses for its main search engine and ranked in order of relevance.

Top ranking strategies - Optimize your data feed and website product pages.

These are recommended shopping bots because of the options they offer merchants, they are high profile and attract a large number of visitors. These are also some shopping bot sites worth looking at -

- Find.com (www.thefind.com/main/AddMerchant.fhtml)
- Live Product Search (http://productupload.live.com/)
- PriceRunner (http://www.pricerunner.com/merchantsignup/signup.html)
- Price.com (http://price.com/add_your_site.html)
- MyTriggers (http://www.mytriggers.com/merchants/merchant_reg.php)
- Nextag (http://www.nextag.com/)
- Ask Shopping (http://sponsoredlistings.ask.com/)
- Amazon Shopping (http://www.amazonservices.com)

C. Things to think about

Using shopping bots is a great way to beef up your website traffic, bringing you qualified shoppers without costing you a lot of money. The most important thing to remember is that not every shopping bot site works in the same way. Choosing the one that suits your product or service will be the success of your ad. If you have a high conversion rate, then a pay-per-click bot can be cost-effective. If your conversion rate is moderate, consider a commission model where you pay only when you make a sale.

A great way to start off is to visit all the shopping bots listed, put yourself in the mindset of a potential customer, and search for your product. This way, you'll be able to check out how products are listed in the search results. This will help you define your unique selling proposition and make your product stand out from the crowd. While shopping bots are an excellent source of cheap, qualified traffic, be sure you don't limit yourself to this one tool. The people using these specialized search engines are in a buying mood and there's no better time to get them to your website so they can buy your products or services.

8. International Orders

A. Looking at international markets

When looking for ways to grow sales and profits, one of the most overlooked techniques is simply expanding your site to target customers in new, untapped markets. International markets are a great way to get your product out in front of a whole new audience. Most people assume that setting up their business to accommodate international buyers will be more trouble than it's worth. While this can sometimes be the case, there are many other instances where expanding into international markets can be a relatively painless way to dramatically increase your bottom line. It's probably not something you'll want to consider until after you've fine-tuned your sales process here at home. If you can't convince people in your own country to buy your product, you're probably not going to fare much better trying to sell to people in the rest of the world.

You should keep in mind that there is a difference between launching a full-scale international marketing effort and simply making your site more accessible to international customers. As long as you don't mind a little extra hassle when it comes to shipping, there is absolutely no reason why you shouldn't accommodate international buyers. If you are selling products that can be delivered electronically then expanding into international markets is a great way to grow your business, as you will be able to instantly bypass the biggest headaches of selling internationally. Since you don't have to send a physical product, you won't have to worry about shipping, customs, etc.

One of the biggest reasons that businesses decide against approaching international markets is the high cost associated with shipping products overseas. The shipping costs are passed on directly to the customer but they often add so much to the final cost that shoppers can usually find a better price from a local company. Depending on the products you are selling, you may find that people will have to pay as much if not more to have an item shipped to them as they do for the actual cost of the item. This scares a lot of customers off at the last minute. There aren't many easy solutions to this problem. Companies like UPS, DHL, and FedEx charge a premium on international shipments to cover their costs, and even using regular mail through the post office can be expensive.

If you have a product that isn't available to the international market from anyone else, this may not be a concern for you. If you are the only distributor for a product that people want, then they may not be concerned about having to pay high shipping costs. If you only sell a few products, you'll want to calculate the shipping costs to various locations and have those figures posted on your ordering page. If you have a large catalog of products, and people are likely to purchase multiple items at once, you'll need to have some kind of shipping calculator posted on your site.

When a product is shipped to someone in another country, there will usually be customs, tax, or duty to be paid on the shipment upon receipt. This is an additional cost that will have to be paid by the customer, and it can be a nasty surprise for them if they aren't expecting it. Make sure you explain about these extra charges somewhere in your order process. This can go a long way towards eliminating angry emails and returns. A great resource for anyone in the US who is considering exporting products is the Small Business Administration's Office of International Trade. This page includes comprehensive how-to information for shipping your company's products overseas.

B. International selling strategies

Selling your products to international markets can create many new revenue streams for your business but this can be difficult to manage from your own country. Once you've established a presence in foreign markets, it could be worth to use some of these selling strategies -

a. International fulfillment houses

If you have been having a lot of success selling your products in a foreign market, you may want to consider working with a local fulfillment house. You could track down a fulfillment house in a European city, and then have them ship your products from a European address, saving your customers a ton in shipping fees. You would still need to ship your products to the fulfillment house, but you could ship a large inventory of your products via container ship and let the fulfillment house ship the orders as they are received. Tracking down a reliable warehousing/shipping/fulfillment company in a foreign country will take some investigating.

b. Local domain name registration

You may want to consider registering your site under a local domain name. If you've decided that you're going to be targeting customers in France, you might try registering a ".fr" domain name. This will make your site that much more appealing to French search engines and will give it a real local flavor. It is important that the organizations that register foreign domain names have different regulations. Some countries will require that you have an address in that country in order to register a local domain name.

c. Affiliate programs

If you are looking for a fast way to break into international markets, your best bet might be to partner with other sites or companies with an established presence in the country you are targeting. The quickest and most effective way to partner up with leading businesses in any country is an affiliate program. If you already have an affiliate program set up, you could have some of your affiliate resources translated into the appropriate language, and start contacting potential partners.

d. International advertising

Marketing your business internationally should really not be much different from marketing your site at home. You can purchase pay-per-click advertising that is targeted to specific countries. One of the best ways to target an international market is to locate popular online newsletters and e-zines based in the region and advertise in them. Many countries have only recently seen their populations start embracing the Internet, you can easily move in and grab the crucial first mover advantage by being the first to make your product available to their market. Tracking down good local advertising resources will be a bit tricky at first, and you'll have to do a lot of testing to see what works with an international audience.

C. Things to think about

When deciding whether or not to venture into international markets, it is important to decide up front how aggressive you are going to be. If you just want to make your product available to be shipped worldwide, you can get away with a lot less work than someone who is serious about competing in a foreign country. Accepting payment from your international customers is a lot easier because companies like PayPal facilitate international payments.

Shipping your products around the world can be a headache, for both you and your customers. The high costs associated with international shipping are one of the biggest barriers to any business's expansion, but there are ways around this problem. Once your international business starts booming, you might want to consider working with a local warehousing company to ship your products out for you.

International markets are a lot more accessible to online businesses than they were a year or two ago. You are now able to purchase pay-per-click advertising you can use to target just about any region on the globe. As more countries start to embrace the Internet for shopping, the possibilities continue to grow.

9. Strategic Alliances

A. What is a strategic alliance?

Any day of the week, you can pick up a business newspaper and read about strategic alliances between countries, governments, universities, mega-corps, big companies, and associations. Strategic alliances are win-win business arrangements that leave all partners smiling. Companies will pay big bucks to have their products worn, driven, eaten, or part of the background, so they can be seen by millions. Some great examples of partnerships include Wal-Mart and Subway, Eddie Bauer and Target, and eBay and Eppraisals.com.

We could go on listing partnerships but we're sure you get the picture. The basic principle of these relationships is always the same, two or more businesses team up and use the other's resources to create new streams of income that would not have been possible on their own. Strategic alliances can be a powerful way to increase your income and these are just a few reasons -

- Strengthen your existing relationship with customers and subscribers by offering them increased value
- A great way to offer new products and services to your existing client and subscriber base
- Give you the perfect opportunity to capitalize on your good name
- Allow you to increase the response you receive by using third-party endorsements
- If you're a reputable business, it should be easy to find other companies to partner with

Your best bet when looking for potential alliances is to hit the search engines and start surfing. You need to be proactive in your approach because, unless you're a well-established business that draws high volumes of targeted traffic to your website, it's unlikely that a deal is just going to drop out of the sky into your lap. Surfing to locate opportunities, researching businesses, and manually recording contact information can be pretty tedious. Your time will be better spent if you can get this done as quickly and painlessly as possible and move on to negotiating the deals. The Alexa toolbar can provide you with the essential information you need about each website you visit. Alexa will tell you -

- How much traffic the site you are viewing receives
- The site owner's personal contact information
- The number of links pointing to a particular site
- Sites that people have surfed to after visiting a particular site

The toolbar gives you the ability to easily and accurately research potential strategic alliance partners, so you'll know which sites and businesses are worth your time and energy. If you use Mozilla's Firefox browser, you can download an extension, called SearchStatus, which will display Alexa rankings and search-related information at www.quirk.biz/searchstatus.

B. Setting up a strategic alliance

Many people are apprehensive about approaching other businesses to suggest a strategic alliance. They are concerned they might be asking too much, or that they might offend someone. Following these steps when setting up your own alliances -

- Contact potential strategic alliance partners personally
- Explain to partners how they will profit from this relationship
- Offer them a sample of your product
- Offer them a special discount to give to their customers
- Take away all the risk
- Make it financially appealing
- Make it extremely easy for them to do
- Get a signed contract that includes the commission terms and everything you have agreed on

Now you be wondering what kind of alliance you should pursue. Here are six simple ideas to get you started -

a. Improve someone's existing marketing campaign

By reading this book you are going to have an Internet marketing education that few have. When you surf the internet, you are going to find yourself noticing common mistakes that businesses are making. You can capitalize on your new-found expertise by offering to work with these sites to improve their marketing strategies for a percentage of the increased sales. There are many businesses that still aren't online. You know how to take these businesses online and profit.

b. Look for two businesses you can pair up to increase both of their profits

In order to set up an alliance like this, you have to look for two key elements -

- An excellent product or service
- An established customer list that will buy the product

Once you've found a good match, your goal is then to negotiate a strategic alliance deal from which everyone will benefit. You'll need to convince the owner of the product that they will achieve higher sales, new customers, and increased profits and you'll need to show the owner of the customer base that the commissions they will earn from the product sales will make their efforts worthwhile. You can earn a nice income simply by showing businesses how to maximize their profits using their existing assets.

c. Talk to your competition

Your competition may have the perfect product or service to complement yours. They may have access to a resource list or market share that you don't. As long as their product is not exactly like yours, you should have little difficulty finding a way to work together.

d. Exchange links or advertising

If both of your sites attract similar traffic, this could be a straight trade and no contracts would be necessary. If they remove your link from their site, you can remove their link from your site. If your sites receive different volumes of traffic, or one site tends to get better quality traffic than the other, you may consider putting together a contract.

C. Things to think about

Strategic alliances are one of the best ways to start earning profits without having either a customer list or a product. You will be amazed when you begin thinking in terms of utilizing and maximizing resources that are already out there.

Chapter Two

Affiliate Programs

1. An Affiliate Program Can Increase Sales

A. What is an affiliate program?

An affiliate program is a referral-based system. Affiliates are people who promote your products on the Internet for a cut of the selling price. Every time they send you a buyer, you pay them a commission. An affiliate program is a simple way to get other people promoting your products for you. It's low maintenance, once you get your program set up, all you have to do is share your marketing materials with your affiliates and send out checks when they make sales. With a few exceptions, almost every product or service online will be much more successful if you offer an affiliate program for it.

Here are four reasons why an affiliate program is a powerful marketing tool -

a. It's a win-win relationship

It's pretty easy to get people to join affiliate programs. They have nothing to lose other than a few hours of their time getting set up. They motivate visitors to click through to your site by posting a banner ad or text link on their website and you do everything else. You lead the visitor through your website, close the sale, process their payment, fulfill their order, and deal with any customer service issues. You track how many orders each affiliate sends you, calculate their commissions, and ensure they get paid what they deserve.

b. No advertising costs

With an affiliate program, you only pay for advertising that gets results. Even if an affiliate has your link up for a year before they make a sale, you don't pay them anything until you make money. It is pretty much no risk advertising.

c. Low risk

Setting up your own affiliate program doesn't have to cost very much at all, if you're prepared to do a lot of the work yourself. The biggest cost will be your time.

d. You can bring new life to your online sales

You have the power to increase your income as more and more affiliates sign up and you continue to teach your existing affiliates how to increase their commission checks. You don't have to go out and spend money on advertising because your affiliates do the advertising for you.

Building an affiliate program is not an overnight process. It will take hard work and a commitment to the success of your business, but it can be worth the effort in the long run. In traditional marketing, referral programs are complicated and time-consuming because it is difficult to track every order. Thanks to affiliate tracking software, managing hundreds of affiliates is easy. There are affordable solutions available that allow you to automatically keep track of which affiliate made which sale. We will share this information with you later.

B. <u>Things to think about</u>

Before you start, you have to know that your affiliate program will only be as successful as your affiliates. It doesn't matter how great your tracking technology is or how carefully you designed and tested your banner ads and text links. If you don't take the time to educate and motivate your affiliates on a regular basis, your program is not going to be very successful. We'll show you what to do to develop a community of excited, motivated affiliates who actively promote your product or service.

2. Start Your Own Program

A. Choosing the right program

When you're setting up, you'll want to decide if you want to create a one-tier or two-tier affiliate program. A one-tier affiliate program, you pay your affiliates a commission for any sales they refer. A two-tier program, you have your regular affiliates, and people have their own sub-affiliates. You pay commissions to affiliates and sub-affiliates.

a. One-tier affiliates

Say your affiliate, Tom, is working for a flat rate commission of $10 for every $79 sale he sends your way. In the first month, he makes 16 sales for you. Here's how it looks -

Tom's sales	16 x $79 = $1264
Tom's commission	16 x $10 = $160
This is your profit	$1264 - $160 = $1104

b. Two-tier affiliates

Now you pay Tom $10 for each sale he sends your way but you also get him to start recruiting his own group of affiliates to sell your product. For every sale made by Tom's sub-affiliates, you'll pay Tom $3 as well as the standard $10 commission to the sub-affiliate who made the sale. In the first month, Tom successfully recruits three new sub-affiliates. Tom makes 16 sales and her sub-affiliates make 3, 5, and 6 sales each. Here's how it works -

	Sales (@ $79 each)	Commissions (@ $10 per sale)
Tom	16	$160
Sub-Affiliate 1	3	$30
Sub-Affiliate 2	5	$50
Sub-Affiliate 3	6	$60
Tom's Sub-Affiliate referral fee ($3 per Sub-Affiliate sale, 14 sales)		$42
TOTAL AFFILIATE FEES PAYABLE		$342
YOUR TOTAL REVENUE	30 x $79	$2,370

THIS GOES IN YOUR POCKET	\$2,370 - \$342	\$2,028

For the same amount of work you made \$2028 as opposed to the \$1104 in sales you made for the single-tier program? That extra \$182 in costs bought you \$1106 in sales and that's not counting the lifetime value of satisfied customers. You will increase your exposure on the Web, as your affiliates recruit affiliates, who recruit more affiliates. This is why you should go one step further when developing your affiliate program by choosing the two-tier model.

B. Pick what you pay for

Once you've figured out if you're going to use a single-tier or two-tier affiliate program, you can pick which kind of profit model you're going to use. If you pay for sales, then you only pay when an affiliate makes a sale. If you pay for clicks, then you pay when an affiliate sends traffic to your website. If you pay for leads, then you pay for each lead sent your way. Each model has advantages and disadvantages, and choosing the best model depends a lot on what kind of a business you have.

a. Pay-per-sale

This is the most popular type of affiliate program. You pay your affiliates a commission on every sale they make. This is the only model that guarantees you will profit, you pay your affiliates only when you make money.

b. Pay-per-click

You pay your affiliates for each person who clicks through to your website from theirs, typical fees paid per visitor range from \$0.01 to \$0.25. Pay-per-click programs carry risk because a click is not a guaranteed sale.

c. Pay-per-lead

You pay your affiliates for each lead they send you. Again, this type of referral is not a guaranteed sale. To use this model effectively, you have to know the value of a lead to your business.

C. Nine tools to help affiliate sales

There are a number of different methods your affiliates can use to persuade people to click through to your website -

a. Email promotions

Email promotions can be a highly profitable promotional technique for your affiliates. Your affiliates have customers and subscribers that trust them and respect their opinions, so when they offer good information about a quality product, their customers will act. It's important to position your product promotions as a personal recommendation. When carrying out email promotions, it's important to take into account CAN-SPAM Act regulations. CAN-SPAM applies to everyone if one of your affiliates is breaking the rules, you could end up paying for it.

b. Text links

Text is the basis of any great website, well-written text can make all the difference when your affiliates are promoting your products. Affiliates can present their visitors with a short sentence or paragraph that clearly explains the benefits of your product, followed by a simple "click here." With this kind of link, it's easy to position a text link as an information resource. Visitors sent to your site by your affiliate are more open to any offer you present them with because they don't feel like they're about to be sold to.

c. Product reviews

Product reviews are consumer opinion pieces that allow your affiliates to subtly endorse your products. One common example of this technique is a book review. Product reviews work because your affiliate offers help and useful information to visitors, instead of just a hard sell. Your affiliates will be happy to give good reviews to your quality products, and their visitors will be more open to buying your products because they've seen them evaluated.

d. E-zine ads

E-zine ads are classified ads designed to be used in your affiliates' email newsletters or e-zines. They're a simple and effective way for your affiliates to promote your products, all they need to do is cut and paste the classified ad into their newsletters, click "Send," and wait for the sales to roll in.

e. Interviews

Interviews are a great way for your affiliates to send you their traffic. Research has shown that people respect the opinions of experts when it comes to what they spend their money on. You can position yourself as an expert by providing your affiliates with a transcript of an interview done with you. Your affiliates can use it as part of an article in their newsletter or on their website. This is a great way to build relationships and credibility.

f. Articles

Articles allow your affiliates to provide their visitors with valuable information, and are a great resource for both your affiliates and their visitors. Articles work well because your affiliates are seen as providing a resource to their visitors, rather than trying to sell to them. Articles are both helpful information and advertising. Each article you distribute to your affiliates will help them to attract more traffic.

g. Banner ads

A banner ad is a graphic link on a website. Instead of clicking underlined blue text to get to a web page, visitors click an image. Banners are designed to entice your target market to click on them. Since they're easy to deploy, they're pretty enticing to affiliates. You provide a choice of graphics and a piece of code and all your affiliate has to do is pick a picture and copy-paste it into their HTML.

h. Hover ads and pop-ups

Hover ads are ads that sit square on top of a web page. They are usually set to appear when you arrive at a website. They are typically designed so that users can't see a website properly until after they have seen the advertisement.

Pop-up ads are similar to hover ads, they appear when you arrive at a website, and usually sit on top of a page's content. The big difference is that pop-ups are hated and all of the major browsers include software that suppresses pop-ups.

i. Product images

Providing your affiliates with product images embedded with their affiliate links gives them all kinds of options. They can use the image on their websites and write personal recommendations to go with it. They can use it in a newsletter and just about anything.

D. Set up commissions

It is important that you pay your affiliates a good commission for each sale they help generate. If you don't, they're not going to be motivated to promote your business. Your affiliates join your program to make money. The higher the commission you can offer them for every sale they refer, the more motivated they'll be to get out there and promote your product or service. Your best affiliates will be the ones who go above and beyond to promote your product or service. They'll be the ones actively promoting your business to their opt-in lists, their newsletter subscribers, visitors to their website, etc...

They won't just post a banner on their site and wait for a sale. The only way people are going to work this hard is if you're recognizing their efforts with a good percentage of the profits you make. The more money they make, the more motivated they will be to market your product or service. A big mistake affiliate program owners make is not recognizing the value of the "backend" sale. They don't understand that people who have bought something from you previously will buy again if you have something similar to offer. If you want to increase your income with your own affiliate program, you need to be prepared to motivate your affiliates by paying good commissions.

You might make minimal profits on the initial sale once you've paid your affiliate and covered your production and fulfillment costs but it's still more profit than you would have earned without that affiliate. Once you've made that first sale, you'll have the opportunity to sell to this person again and again. The only way to understand if you have a great commission payout is to talk with your affiliates. If they're happy with it, then you're set.

E. Things to think about

Starting your own affiliate program is your ticket to performance-based advertising because you only ever pay for results. You can sign up hundreds of affiliates who will promote your product or service to their customers, newsletter subscribers, opt-in email lists, etc. You set the rules regarding how your affiliates are allowed to market your products, and you only pay them when they make a sale. A two-tier affiliate program lets you take the process one step further by motivating your affiliates to recruit sub-affiliates of their own.

3. Your Affiliate Program on Autopilot

A. Outsource or do it yourself

There are affordable solutions available that allow you to automatically keep track of which affiliate made which sale, where each customer is coming from, exactly how much you owe each affiliate and all the other details you need to know. One of the most important decisions you will make when starting your own affiliate program is whether you will manage the program yourself or outsource it to an affiliate management service.

a. Outsourcing

If you have a bigger budget to work with and you're not interested in running your program yourself, then you may want to consider outsourcing your affiliate program to a management service like -

- Commission Junction
- LinkShare
- ClickBank

These companies will look after details like recruiting affiliates, tracking affiliate sales, and writing your checks each month. The costs of these services are far beyond the startup budget of a small or home-based business. Commission Junction charges a startup fee of around $2,250, and LinkShare charges $5,000. That's just the start up. ClickBank's program charges a $49.95 activation charge, but 7.5% commission that comes straight out of your profits plus a flat $1 charge per product sold. All these programs take a percentage of the sales you make, ranging anywhere from 4% to 50%.

Outsourcing your affiliate program might seem to make sense at first. You need to be aware that with the techniques and strategies you're learning, you'll be able to grow your affiliate program quickly. You may find yourself handing over a very large portion of your profits to your solution provider. Outsourcing might be the way to go if you're planning to keep your program small. Switching over to an in-house program will be extremely difficult if you change your mind or if your program takes off. This is a serious decision you need to make right from the start.

b. Do it yourself

There are a number of reasons to run your affiliate program yourself -

- You don't have to pay the startup costs that are involved in outsourcing your program. Just the one-time cost of affiliate software and you keep control of your program.

- When you run your affiliate program, you keep 100% of the profits after you pay your affiliates.
- You have 100% control over when and how you promote your affiliate program, who joins, who does not, your payment structure, your commissions, and every promotion you do.

The startup costs and percentage of your profits that you're required to pay out just don't make outsourcing your affiliate program worth the trouble.

B. Track your affiliates

If your affiliates aren't confident they're receiving credit for each and every sale they send you, they aren't going to be your affiliates for very long. That's why it's important to have a well-designed tracking system in place. There are three common ways to do this -

a. Tracking through HTML

Using this method, you would set up a separate website for each of your affiliates. This is a time-consuming way to do things but there are almost no costs involved other than your time. This method can start to get out of control quickly, if you're trying to market multiple products. Your workload increases as more and more affiliates join. If your time is worth anything and you're planning on running a successful affiliate program with more than a couple of affiliates, avoid this option. The only benefit to HTML is that it's cheap to implement if you're short on cash and have a lot of time on your hands. It may not be the most professional way to go, and potential affiliates will be turned off by the lack of real-time statistics but some sort of affiliate program is better than no program.

b. CGI tracking

Tracking programs that use CGI scripting put the affiliate's code right in the URL as the referred visitor is surfing through your site. The code is visible to the visitor because it becomes part of the URL. These URLs can get long, as the affiliate code isn't hidden, but displayed right in the URL. If someone leaves your site, but remembers your domain name without the affiliate identification there is no way to track the visitor and give the referring affiliate credit for the sale. You'll find that some people will notice the long URL with a lot of "codes" in it. They'll erase the extra codes in the URL and go back to the root domain to see if there is something different there.

Because the affiliate identification number appears directly in the URL, it's obvious to many of your visitors that they're being tracked. The visitor can only be tracked if they're coming directly from the affiliate's site. If the visitor leaves and comes back later to buy, you have no way of knowing that an affiliate originally referred them.

c. Cookie tracking

A cookie is a tiny bit of information that a website puts on your hard drive so it will remember who you are when you come back to visit later. The cookie will identify which affiliate sent you which visitor, which makes it much easier to track their sales. It doesn't matter if the visitor decides to purchase right away, or comes back weeks or months later to buy the cookie stays with them and the affiliate always gets credit. If the visitor clicks on your order form, your affiliate software program will check the affiliate identification number in the cookie and use it to track the sale.

When the sale goes through, the affiliate's sale counter is increased by one so that the affiliate can see in real time exactly how many sales they have. This means that your affiliates will get credit for all the sales they make and that means you'll have happy affiliates who trust you. The cookies make it easy to track the visitors from affiliate links because no matter how many products a visitor orders. You will find that cookie tracking makes your affiliate program an easy sell to potential affiliates, as you can tell them they will be credited for all of their sales. You can assure them that whether their referred visitors choose to buy immediately or wait it doesn't matter.

Offline orders are all the orders made through other channels than your online ordering system. These purchases will always happen, as some people aren't comfortable ordering over the Internet. You need to be prepared to track your affiliate sales by phone, fax, and mail. It's something that not many affiliate programs do and it's a good way to set yourself above your competition. Cookies can actually be used to track both of these orders. You can code your order form to include the affiliate identification number to appear as a suite number or a publication number. That way when the offline orders come in you can track which affiliate has made the sale.

C. Questions to ask before choosing a provider

The point of setting up an affiliate program is to make it easy for the affiliate to join and send you qualified visitors. This means that as an affiliate program owner, you need to choose software or a service that will not only take a lot of the work out of your hands, but also make it easy for your affiliates to join and get all of the information they need to be successful. You shouldn't worry about how the software or service works or how you're going to integrate it with your existing website. Whatever you choose should be easy to implement and customize. There's a lot of software out there but a lot of them are not worth your money.

In addition to the cost of the affiliate program software, there are a few other out-of-pocket costs that you will encounter -

- Hosting fees
- Costs for any kind of modifications
- Maintenance, updates, or anything special

Remember that as long as you choose your affiliate software wisely, the costs should be minimal. It is more cost-effective to have your own affiliate software, have 100% control, and be able to make special modifications to it if you want to add features or customize it for your business. Before buying here are some questions you should ask -

a. Is the affiliate sign-up process fully automated?

You should make it clean and easy for affiliates to join. When your prospective affiliate fills out the sign-up form, you should be able to automatically send them everything they need to get started and it should all happen without you doing anything.

b. Is there an automated contact system?

Make sure that you can automatically email all your affiliates if you want. All it should take is a click of a button to send them an email that updates them on what is happening and how they can earn even higher commission checks.

c. Does it offer flexible administrative functions?

Your administrative functions should work for you. Can you call up a web page and check to see how all your affiliates are doing? Can you go into the software and make adjustments? Does the program give you monthly commission reports? Can you make instant changes to all affiliate sites? The software you choose should have the ability to do all of this for every affiliate with the push of a few buttons.

d. Does affiliate tracking happen automatically?

Good software will track through all different types of browsers, setups, and visitors. It will track orders, whether they are made online or whether they come through an 800 number order, by fax, or by regular mail. Your software should be able to track all visitors, whether they order today, tomorrow, or a year from now, no matter how many products or services they order.

e. Can you offer variable payouts?

It's important that you have software that allows you to choose to pay a fixed amount per click-through, a fixed amount per sale, or a percentage of the sale. You need to be in charge of determining your payout.

f. Are you able to get real-time statistics?

You want real-time statistics. Your affiliates should be able to check their sales statistics any time they want by visiting your affiliate resource center, entering their username and password, and viewing their own personal sales statistics page. They should be able to see how many visitors they are sending over and how many of their visitors are being converted into paying customers. This allows them to test various sales techniques at their site to see what works well for them.

g. Can you count each affiliate's referred visitor and sales separately?

Make sure you have software that will count the number of visitors and the number of sales for each affiliate separately. That way, you can see which affiliates are sending you quality visitors and which are not. With this information, you'll know who your top affiliates are, as well as who might need some help improving their visitor-to-sales conversion ratio.

h. Are the minimum payout settings flexible?

You should be able to preset your check payout levels. Don't set this amount too high, as affiliates who have low sales will get frustrated and may drop your program.

i. Does it manage automated check paying?

The affiliate program software that you choose should be able to automatically write the checks to your affiliates. This might not seem important but as you get bigger and start having to write more checks. You will want a way to automate this. The software automatically downloads all of the affiliates' personal information along with the exact amount that we owe them in referral fees for that month. This means that you can easily load this information into your accounting software and print checks.

There are many small things that the software should automatically look that you haven't even considered yet. Some software not only writes all the checks but also prints out the stats for each affiliate, prints out mailing labels etc. There are many different affiliate management systems out there and the best way to find one is to do a google search with these questions in mind. One we have found is iDefAffiliate. With this you can -

- Automatic approval of new affiliate accounts
- Contact all of your affiliates via email.
- Check up on your affiliates' progress, or change your marketing strategy
- Keep track of where orders come from
- Set your own payouts and change them whenever you like
- Real-time stats for you and for your affiliates
- Detailed statistics about traffic from affiliates
- Set your own minimum payout
- Automatically pay your affiliates

The Standard Edition costs $99.99, Gold Edition $199.99 and a Platinum Edition for $299.99.

D. Things to think about

You'll need to plan to manage your affiliate program effectively and automatically. Manual solutions may work when your affiliate program is small but as you recruit more affiliates, you'll find yourself spending countless hours on chores. The good part is that automating your affiliate program is easy and there is software available that makes managing many affiliates as easy as managing one. You want to be able to focus on recruiting new affiliates to bring in more income, not manually tracking orders and writing checks.

4. Recruit, Manage, and Reward

A. Screening your affiliates

Your affiliate program will only be as successful as your affiliates. It doesn't matter how sophisticated your tracking technology is, or how carefully you designed and tested your banner ads and text links. If you don't take the time to educate and motivate your affiliates, your program won't be successful. There are two ways to build an affiliate program.

a. Mass-recruiting

There's nothing wrong with opening your affiliate program to anyone who wants to join just make sure you cultivate real relationships with your best affiliates. If you do choose to go this route, you're playing the numbers game. Your objective is to sign up as many affiliates as possible because you know that for every 100 or so you may have one amazing affiliate who will make you money. The problem with this is as possible is the majority of people who sign up for your affiliate program will have little experience marketing. Some of them will join every affiliate program they find and turn their website into a flea market, while others may get only a handful of visitors.

If you decide to go with mass recruitment there are different to make this work -

a. Actively recruit affiliates by searching the Web

You need to have a clear idea of who your target market is. It is critical that you know this because good affiliates will be those who have direct access to these people. Once you know who your target market is, it's easy to figure out where they hang out and which businesses would be perfect affiliates. One of the best ways to do this is by acting like a customer and searching your keywords in one of the major search engines. Make a note of what sites keep coming up, these are the businesses you'll approach to join your program.

b. Promote to your customers and subscribers

This can be an effective way to recruit affiliates because these people have experience with your products and services. They know you, they know your products, and they obviously have a sincere interest in your industry.

c. Find high-traffic sites that are selling advertising space

There are a lot of sites with advertising space that is unused, one technique is to persuade these sites to post your affiliate banner or text link. You can tell them that if it works well for them, they may find the affiliate link makes them more money than their regular advertising.

d. Advertise in newsletters and e-zines

E-zines and online newsletters are excellent places to advertise your affiliate program. You should pick e-zines that are reputable and that you think reach the right market for your products or services.

e. Register your program with affiliate program directories

It's a good idea to register your affiliate program with the major affiliate program directories, this is where a lot of people search when they're looking for a program to join. Some directories include -

- Associate Programs (http://www.associateprograms.com/)
- Affiliates Directory (http://www.affiliatesdirectory.com/)

The list of affiliate directories for you to submit your program is growing quickly. The ones listed above are the ones worth submitting to first.

f. Do business with your competitors

You wouldn't believe how often your competitors will end up being your top affiliates. Your competitors are the people who have direct access to your target market and they often have a customer base or opt-in lists that are comparable to yours.

g. Actively promote your program

Don't limit yourself to the promotion techniques listed. Think creatively and recruit affiliates by getting on the phone and connecting with potential affiliates, approaching through email, participating in forums and commenting on blog posts, encouraging your affiliates to tell their friends and colleagues about your program and anything else you can think of.

The best way to recruit new affiliates is to make your sign-up process quick and easy. If potential affiliates have to fill out six different forms and wait three days for approval you'll risk losing them. It's worth automating your affiliate program using a system which has been built to automatically manage an unlimited number of affiliates. It allows your affiliates to sign up on a simple web form, and their information is automatically entered into your database.

b. Super Affiliates

If you want to keep your affiliate program small and administrative chores to a minimum, then you may want to screen the applicants. This gives you the power to choose affiliates who have sites that closely relate to your target market. You can recruit a small team of powerful affiliates who generate a lot of sales for your website. And you won't have to worry about the administrative tasks that come with a larger affiliate program. The downside to searching and screening applicants is that it takes time. The approval process involves work, as you will need to check out the applicant's website, ask how they plan to promote your program, etc... It pays off in the long run, these super affiliates can become very valuable business partners with the potential to increase your revenue. Here's how you can find out where they're hiding -

a. Search the Web

You need to know your target market inside out before searching for super affiliates. This way, you'll be able to identify websites that cater to the same audience. You should follow the same online search for a mass-recruitment. Use search engines and online directories to find sites that are aimed at a similar target market to yours. When you look for super affiliates, you need to focus on the sites that appear right at, or near, the top of your search results. These sites are ones most likely to be run by people with the right combination of Web savvy and business experience. Unlike mass-recruitment your search for super affiliates concentrates on quality not quantity.

b. Dig deeper to find your top performers

Once you've located some good prospects, you need to build up a full picture of their business, the level of traffic their website gets, and who their target audience is. You have to make sure they are targeting the same people as you, and that they have enough traffic to be able to generate good sales. You can ask them these things but it's better to do some investigating. You can dig deeper using these tools-

- Google Toolbar (www.google.com/toolbar)
- Alexa Toolbar (http://download.alexa.com/index.cgi)
- LinkPopularity (www.linkpopularity.com)
- Ranking (www.ranking.com)

These resources will enable you to build up a profile of your potential super affiliate's website, and provide you with enough information to make the decision on whether to approach them or not.

c. Learn to identify super affiliates

Super affiliates share certain characteristics that make them stand out. To save you time wading through the information you'll get using the tools, you need to know how to pinpoint these characteristics. Here are some things to look for -

- Do they have a good website?
- Does their product or service relate to the theme of your website?
- Do they focus on just one product (or group of products)?
- Do they understand Internet marketing?
- Do they drive tons of targeted traffic to their website?
- Do they have an opt-in email list?
- Do they send out a regular newsletter?

After identifying suitable candidates for your affiliate program, the next step is to make contact and convince them it's in their best interest to promote your products. Here's a good way to make contact -

- Call them first and explain who you are and how they could benefit from joining your program
- Follow up with a personalized email, explaining exactly who you are and what you do. Then direct them to your affiliate program page
- About a week later if they don't respond to your first email, send a reminder email.
- Follow up with each potential affiliate two more times, reminding them that you have already contacted them and letting them know that you're interested in doing business with them.

When a potential affiliate approaches you, the first question on their mind is, "What's in it for me?" You have to answer this question as quickly as you can. Tell them that your product is of high quality and in demand. Tell them how much money they can make and how easy it is for them to get involved. Make sure you are offering high enough commissions. When you approach people and ask them to become your affiliate, they will have questions like -

- Will it cost me anything to be involved?
- How long does it take to get set up?
- How long will it take for my application to be processed?
- When do I get paid?
- Is there a minimum check amount that is sent out?
- Are graphics or banners provided?
- Can I get information on visitors and sales?
- How often can I access my sales statistics?

These are the kinds of things you want to go over with new affiliates. You also want to make it clear that you take care of all the credit card charges, shipping the product, handling customer service, and all the administration.

B. Tools for building relationships

It is important to stay in regular contact with your affiliates. Let them know about what is selling and what is working. You know your business best, it's your job to come up with slogans and text links for your affiliates to use. You should test different ones and then let your affiliates know which ones generate the highest sales. Showing them what works is a large part of motivating an affiliate to take the steps necessary to build a great referral business. Educating and motivating your affiliates is an important part of your job and should be one of your top priorities. You should make sure that as soon as an affiliate signs up for your program, send them a welcome email that directs them to your Affiliate Resource Center, where they can find all of the information and materials they need to get started.

a. Affiliate welcome letter

Your welcome letter is an important part of your program's success. This should be where you guide your affiliates, step-by-step, through the process of selling your product. You should provide your affiliates with linking instructions, tips and tricks for maximizing their sales, and links to any resources that you believe will be of value to them when getting started. Tell them what promotion methods you have found most effective and how you will support them in using these methods.

b. Frequently Asked Questions page

Your Frequently Asked Questions page will save you a lot of time if you set it upright. Your goal is to anticipate all the questions your affiliates may have and provide them with clear answers. The more questions you can answer on your page, the less time you'll be forced to spend emailing back and forth with your affiliates. Once you start receiving questions from your affiliates, you'll be able to adjust your FAQ page to better meet your affiliate's needs.

c. Articles that contain marketing tips

New affiliates should have access to articles and promotional tools designed to give them specific tips and tricks for increasing their sales.

d. Affiliate Newsletter

An affiliate newsletter not only allows you to keep in regular contact with your affiliates, it gives you a good opportunity to motivate them by providing the latest, most profitable tips and tricks for promoting your product or service. Your affiliate newsletter should be sent on a regular basis, whether it's once a month, once every two months, or even once every three months. Tell them what they need to know to promote new products or take part in a new promotion, then give them the tools to start selling.

Every affiliate who signs up will be different. Different websites, different markets, different motivations, different levels of experience marketing and different work ethics. This means that the sales they generate are going to vary. Some affiliates will read about your program, get excited, sign up, and never take the necessary steps to link to your website and start generating sales. Some affiliates will sign up for your program and try promoting your product or service to a market that has absolutely no interest. These affiliates might generate one or two sales but will never be anything outstanding.

Some affiliates will promote to a market with a direct interest in your product or service. They'll never do much more than post a text link on their website, so their sales will be average. Your super affiliates will go all out to promote your product or service, using every technique they can think of to increase their affiliate sales.

C. Things to think about

Starting and developing your own affiliate program is no task. There are a lot of important steps and decisions that need to be considered if you want to take full advantage of this marketing strategy. With your own program you can -

- Reduce your advertising costs
- Increase your recognition by increasing your exposure
- Increase the effectiveness of your advertising
- Increase your customer base and increase your income

Recruiting and managing affiliates takes time and effort, it's worth using software to do the work for you. Software can sign up new affiliates and get them started automatically while they're still fresh and eager to work with you.

In Closing

We hope you enjoyed this book and can use what we've shared to continue to grow your business. If you did not write down the links we shared with you throughout this book don't worry. Just visit the helpful links pdf provided on your bonus CD. Bear in mind Internet Marketing is always changing and some of the ideas, techniques, services, policies ect., in this book might have changed before we get a chance to update it.

If you haven't yet I urge you read "Rookie Mistakes In Online Business Anyone Can Learn". If you don't you will be missing out on valuable information that will save you time and money. If you are having trouble, have questions, or are interested in learning more about a particular marketing technique.

Please contact us at - takteam@ourgrnbusiness.com.

Thank You!

Kristin and Tom

Made in the USA
Monee, IL
08 November 2026

67381745R10037